MW00531978

Uncanny Valley

CLEVELAND STATE UNIVERSITY POETRY CENTER

NEW POETRY

Michael Dumanis, Series Editor

Samuel Amadon, *The Hartford Book*
John Bradley, *You Don't Know What You Don't Know*
Lily Brown, *Rust or Go Missing*
Elyse Fenton, *Clamor*
Emily Kendal Frey, *The Grief Performance*
Dora Malech, *Say So*
Shane McCrae, *Mule*
Helena Mesa, *Horse Dance Underwater*
Philip Metres, *To See the Earth*
Zach Savich, *The Firestorm*
Sandra Simonds, *Mother Was a Tragic Girl*
S. E. Smith, *I Live in a Hut*
Mathias Svalina, *Destruction Myth*
Allison Titus, *Sum of Every Lost Ship*
Liz Waldner, *Trust*
Allison Benis White, *Self-Portrait with Crayon*
Jon Woodward, *Uncanny Valley*

For a complete listing of titles please visit
www.csuohio.edu/poetrycenter

Uncanny Valley

poems

Jon Woodward

Cleveland State University Poetry Center
Cleveland, Ohio

Copyright © 2012 by Jon Woodward

All rights reserved
Printed in the United States of America
Printed on acid-free paper

ISBN 978-1-880834-99-2

First edition

5 4 3 2 1

This book is published by Cleveland State University Poetry Center,
2121 Euclid Avenue, Cleveland, Ohio 44115-2214
www.csuohio.edu/poetrycenter and is distributed
by SPD/Small Press Distribution, Inc. www.spdbooks.org.

Cover image: *Tempura*, 2004, 80.5 x 80.5 cm acrylic on canvas, © Hideaki
Kawashima, courtesy of Tomio Koyama Gallery.

Uncanny Valley was designed and typeset by Amy Freels in Joanna with Alternate
Gothic No 2 display.

LIBRARY OF CONGRESS CATALOGING-IN-PUBLICATION DATA
Woodward, Jon, 1978–
  Uncanny valley : poems / Jon Woodward. — 1st ed.
    p. cm.
  "Winner of the 2011 Cleveland State University Poetry Center Open
Competition."
  ISBN 978-1-880834-99-2 (alk. paper)
  I. Title.

PS3623.O685U53 2012
811'.6—dc23

2011047849

Acknowledgments

My sincere thanks to the editors of the following journals, for originally publishing poems or sections of poems from this collection, sometimes in a slightly or significantly different form: *At-Large, Barrow Street, BOMBlog, Catch Up, The Laurel Review,* and *Saltgrass.*

I would also like to offer profound thanks to Ian Dreiblatt, for the conversation.

Finally, my very profoundest thanks and love to Oni Buchanan, for wholeheartedness and everything and everything.

Contents

Uncanny Valley

Huge Dragonflies

Huge dragonflies aim at your face.
Hope dwells eternally there.
Hope dwells eternally there.
Sound waves define characterist
istics of every interpersonal action
Hope dwells eternally there.
Hope dwells eternally there.
Hope dwells eternally there.
Hope dwells eternally there.
Hope dwells eternally
Enough food not enough food
Hope dwells eternally there
Hope dwells eternally there.
The sound of a calm fizz
breaks and dissipates
with a touch on the bl
ind girl's shoulder to
congratulate her, her exhalation
tion Hope dwells eternally there
Hope dwells eternally there
Hope dwells eternally there
Hope dwells eternally there
in an electromagnetic static
which never dulls or sharpens
Hope dwells eternally there

Hope dwells eternally there
Hope dwells eternally there
Hope dwells eternally there
Hope dwells eternally there
Hope dwells eternally there
The fires have been put out
weeks ago, & the insects
have moved into the area
and are chewing it apart audibly
Hope dwells eternally there.
Hope dwells eternally there.
This election has really given
these people something to look
Hope dwells eternally there.
Hope dwells eternally there.
Hope dwells
The portcullis is ratcheted
back open, silent tourists
Hope dwells eternally there and
sine waves take shape away
from every interpersonal interaction,
an imposition from above Hoo
ooope dwell there eternally
Hopes dwell there eternally
Hopes dwell there eternally
Hopes dwell there eternally
From me. From me, From me
Hopes dwell there eternally

Hopes dwell there eternally
Hopes dwell there eternally
Hopes dwell there eternally
Hopes dwell there eternally
Hopes dwell there eternally
Hopes dwell there eternally
Hopes dwell there eternally
Hopes dwell there
in a never dulled and never
jammed audio static.
Hopes dwell there eternally
Hopes dwell there eternally.
A simple notching machine marks
the progress of a plastic
manufacturing that shuts off
cuts off an identicalt
twin succubus halfway
out the window
Hope dwells there eternally.
Dwell dwell there eternally
because there fire in the hearts
has never gone out Hope
Hope dwells there eternally
Hope dwells there eternally
Hope dwells there eternally
Hope dwells there eternally
Hope dwells there eternally
Hope dwells there eternally

Hope dwells there eternally
Hope dwells there eternally.
Hope dwells there eternally.
Hope dwells there eternally.
Hope dwells there eternally.
Hope dwells there eternally.
Hope dwells there eternally.
Hope dwells there eternally.
Hope dwells there eternally.
Hope has a hard pair of fing
ernails claw open the sound
Gigantic manufact
Gigantic manufact
Gigant manufacturing equipment fall
ing over to put a huge crash
on tape and secure a grant
to feed the soul of the listener
or claw away, an extra antenna where
the finger was. Who would rather
feed somewhere else. She went blind
from it, from it
Hope dwells eternally there
Hope dwells eternally there
Hope dwells eternally there
Hope dwells eternally there
Hope dwells eternally there
Hope dwells eternally there
Hope dwells eternally there

Hope dwells eternally there
Hope dwells eternally there
Hope dwells eternally there
Hope dwells eternally there
Hope dwells eternally there
Hope dwells eternally there.
Hope dwells eternally there.
Hope dwells eternally there.
Hope dwells eternally there.
Hope dwells eternally there.
The wood-boring beetles and
gall-wasps and wood grubs,
the ants and formic acid
Hope dwells eternally the
little legs traversing any surface
or oaring the ocean waves and
wasp abdomens marking like star
charted points the islands
stung into the rower's back.
Hope dwells eternally there.
Hope dwells eternally there.
Hope dwells eternally, trailing
a parachute there
Hopes dwell eternally there.
Hopes dwell eternally there.
Hopes dwell eternally there.
Hopes dwell eternally there.
Hopes dwell eternally there.

Hopes dwell eternally there.
Hopes dwell eternally there.
Hopes dwell eternally there.
Hopes dwell eternally there.
Hopes dwell eternally there.
Hopes dwell eternally there.
Hopes dwell eternally there.
Hopes dwell eternally there.
Hopes dwell eternally there.
Hopes dwell eternally there.
Hopes dwell eternally there.
Hopes dwell eternally there.
Hopes dwell eternally there.
Hopes dwell eternally there.
Hopes dwell eternally there.
Hopes dwell eternally there.
Thick men bang wads of keys
against hard surfaces there.
Hopes dwell eternally there.
Hopes dwell eternally there.
Hopes dwell eternally there.
Hopes dwell eternally there.
Hopes dwell eternally there.
Hopes dwell eternally there.
Hopes dwell eternally there.
Hopes dwell eternally there.
Hopes dwell eternally there.
Hopes dwell eternally there.

Hopes dwell eternally there.
Hopes dwell eternally there.
Hopes dwell eternally there.
Hopes dwell eternally there
Hopes dwell eternally there
Hopes dwell eternally there
Hopes dwell eternally there
Hopes dwell eternally there
Hopes dwell eternally there
Hopes dwell eternally there
Hopes dwell eternally there
Hopes dwell eternally there
Hopes dwell eternally there
Hopes dwell eternally there
Hopes dwell eternally there
Hopes dwell eternally there
Hopes dwell eternally there
Hopes dwell eternally there
Hopes dwell eternally there
Hopes dwell eternally there
Hopes dwell eternally there
Hopes dwell eternally there
Hopes dwell eternally there
Hopes dwell eternally there
Hopes dwell eternally there
Hopes dwell eternally there

Killing Flies Skyscraper Figurine

Not sky blue or powder blue
Or baby blue or robin's egg blue,
The thought of Killing Flies
Starts to be written in you.

In what blue are its mirrors, and what
Girders write in its shadow down, and
Reflected, whose mirror reflects them?
A tiny friend of me who looks like me

Or rolls back the rolling contours of the lens? Or not
Lens the contours are wrapped around a
Lens of the contours wrapped around?
Write down all their deaths, slam

The flesh of his hands together
A deified sound, a thunderbolt
To whom, and under what blue
What light wrapped around the lens the

Girders wrapped around a
Lens of the girders wrapped around
A lens of the girders wrapped around?
And this is how I should feel

No listen, no never listen, no pause
& listen, & never, never listen, no these
Dots before my eyes and in my eyes should
Should, should feel, should

The Half Horse

The transporter gateway goes
Where the other half of the horse
Is hidden. Electric charge flows
Through the gateway
Keeping it closed through
The horse where this flank is.
It would be a remarkable thing to know
Where horse muscle does come from.
The gateway goes & goes.
Money (more money than you've ever seen)
Keeps it there, but closed
In a round, enclosed room
And nothing is seen through it.

This horse, charging. This horse's muscles
Rippling and quaking, thunder accumulating
Somewhere, steam
Fearsome breathing
Located in the internal understanding of its body.
The overpowering galloping of mustangs
On the high plains of Utah, near enough to the Interstate
To be seen. Government

The half horse closes a circuit,
Current flows to & from
The gateway and the wall outlet
Through this half a horse.
A circular gateway shut
(does transporter gateway technology exist yet? I don't know)
Current
Opens closes a shutter
So to speak. Oh gawd
Rifle butt. Ass
This is me on guard duty
[photo]   Anyways, uhh,
So, it's cumbersome to arrange
A half horse and keep it closed.
And so expensive! The government

Power cuts and the gateway opens
Looking back out at me
On guard duty. I don't recognize
He holds away his own hand
As though attempting to protect
Against his mirror image
The 18-year-old with the fool's face
The 64-year-old breaker of horses
A conscripted look flows through
From somewhere, through his mare eyes
Completing a circuit
Well, forget it I can't remember.

Something or someone drew my chariot
Through a very distant story,
Participating in a horse's human war
I threw a spear through
(Watching me through the gateway throw, no recollection)

And with a thud
No spear falls out of the gateway
No narrative momentum

Aesthetic experiences are all I have.
Every step forward under the bare, icy tree branches
Forces their pattern to re-overlap and re-render.
I burn my hand or I run my hand
Under cold water. I walk my hand around
In freezing February, I fold up some origami
And I cut the vegetables for dinner and I retrace
And I try to retrace my thoughts and other people's thoughts.
They'll look back through the gateway
And instead of aesthetic experiences
They'll see mostly first-person pronouns
Snuck through the gate in a false horse.
They snuck themselves back in
The future. They're silent

~ ~ ~

Put my hand
Outside a real horse.

Revision amasses themselves
The rioter's one word and arm is
Designed to fade into unreason
The homemade shield
Revision will never touch
Revision will touch it and
Change it there. The Congress Building
Comes down of itself.
The name burns
Outward the spiral pattern
Upon waking. Wake
The excrement of the dream
Punch numbers. The name
Said opposite oneself
Into the telephone microphone
In the telecommunications era
Awoken at street level the
Elevator held to the head
Floods open with people

Enunciation extends into their
Midst a hyperbridge.
A word and no other words
Unconnected to every other word.

A word to tell themselves
The name, the question of it
Bypassing it. Not the word
Itself. Nothing there
The memory gate opens onto a nothing
No memorysiege
No rhymesiege.

A bridge past the unbreachable
Aging
The word itself.
Steam
Yelling into a steamcloud

Striking their heads and feet
Against the bridge abutment,
Stubbing blindly, madly
In retromotivic search of it,
The (their) magic word.
Simple. Name
Simply enunciation
Simply an enunciation

Heard, Half-Awake, August 14th, 2009

(out loud, repeat each pair of lines six times or so)

I don't think I nee no
because the whole thing bear wathpth

～ ～ ～

enton very like that,
a separay mmm

～ ～ ～

overhere what's a gains brothers
and I don't get anymore

～ ～ ～

p'sing this beautiful day
& no wrzy a shzlike

～ ～ ～

this guy, he absolutely
zen a terremite shiver down my neck

～ ～ ～

that's great! wholly double bogger
and totally-worth-it-but-you-know-I-heard

Between Identical Cities (A Reminder)

Until the heart dissolves into the bloodstream,
As city walls and tunnels slump and dissolve
With the sudden return of the river
To its ancient bed

~ ~ ~

Echoing, echoing, as he sang.

My captor sang inside my voice
And inside his I crawled and broke
and break the bloodstream, hang the raindrops,
round, and in between us, spoke

the turning of audiotape inside-out,
a sandstone canyon a person squeezes
down, into, out of the sunshine
(the moment your eyes need to adjust)

A dark and dark red sandstone canyon
acting as a natural aqueduct
between the old city and the new city
(the echo of running water)

Salamander

The janitor asked me
how to pronounce the creature's name
& I said salamander for him.

He looked at it on the screen
and I looked at him.

Slide your legs into its tail I said.
I can't he said as he did.
Feed your guts there into its cavity

of guts, I can't he said (manifestly untrue
because he did). Mash the thing's
name and yours I said together into

that irreversible hole I know you keep
and he did & it broke over his face

& flowed, water from the earth,
I can't, I can't, he said.

Uncanny Valley

Push the remote button and
The mechanical brayer brays

Lines notated like the previous two
Are repeated (as a pair)
As many times as the reader desires,
From zero to 255, before continuing.

Similar notation, applied to one word only,
Sometimes |drives down the middle of a line.

The better part of a long drive
Is the most important meal of the bray.

The reader reads aloud,
And the driver drives

Ancient desert robots
Ancient desert robots
Robots of ancient device
Robots of ancient device
Sent seven huge trees
Down onto the motorway
Up onto the overpass
Seven trees landed on there
To kill any and all abominations.

Uprooted trees
Need gravity so bad
Need gravity so bad

Or they get nostrils and |eyes confused

And all abominations were in a car accident
You can't make them out from here,
The facial muscles fade out
Over the distance

The face figures out
Of the distance
Leaving featureless mask
Leaving featureless mask

They totaled
Seven cars, seven bodies
Seven mask, seven muscles
Seven trees, fpushed over
Seven trees, on them

They escaped the wreck and were free
They got free of the wreck
There was no more wreck, there!
And they walked upon the earth.

And their shadows insisted upon wax
They were a wax statue upon
One was a wax doll upon
One was a paraffin vampire upon
Wax upon

Their shadows clogged up the wax sun
Their shadows clogged up the wax sun

They ree a wax statue
They roo a wax statue
They raa a wax statue

What thoughts wreck thoughts
Could I rubberneck those
What thoughts rubberneck thoughts
Could I wreck those

These thoughts are best left
To Ouagadougou's bougainvilleas
They thought

How can I think such things
I have the outrage
An outrage of wax

That's what it is
An outrage of wax

That's what I say
An outrage of wax

Hot

Raw

Gross

They climbed back in the car wreck and had lunch.

Seven in all they made.

They split off and formed pairs one by one.

A seven-sided star made of knuckles.

A seven-sided star make of knuckles
A seven-sided star kmake of knuckles

I'm like, knuckles and Kevin and wax
I'm like, knuckles and Kevin and wax

Give kback to fissile ribbon figurine?
Give kback to fissile ribbon fkigurine?

Visible fissile ribbons
Visible fissile ribbons
Went through the blood and
Came out the nostrilf

Don't rubberneck a wreck
Don't gape at an ape
Don't spy on a guy
etc., whatever

Thousands of cars poured onto the motorway
To see the wreck.
It was the wrong way to go about it!

Don't try to look at the wreck

Stay
Off the moto
Wray

Much later, it all got sorted out
The desert was hot all directions
The breaffast was nourishing paste
The sun was considered an ancient and important symbol

The sun was too bright
To be a symbol, so it wasn't.

The flying snake learned to extend its ribs laterally
To form a failure to fear falling.

Driving upon the underside of a flying snake in flight
Driving upon considered the underside of a snake in flight

To form a gliding surface

During lunch they had breaffast
During breaffast they got in a car wreck
It turned out, much later,
That there were seven victims
They were okay, then
Not a scratch on them
They began to complain of maladies
My heart only absorfs wax sun one said and
My heart only absorfs wax sun one said and

Seven of them decided, Safety First!
But their ancient Lord and Creator
Heaved up from the Valley of Deepest Being
A septet of trees
Which landed inside the pathways of their brains
Which were hardwired for the steering of cars

And from that day forward
He placed a big robot in the sky
To remind them
Of
Love.

There was this like pipe
Like a plumbing pipe
Protruding periloufly ou
Wha tha fee fa, oo fee thla,
Fla frosthetic folphin spout
Out the upper part of the head
After the wreck
There were feven |fpoutf
There were feven fpoutf
There were of seven of spouts |of
There were of seven of spouts |of

Okay

And

"Lion you bed down with a heavy heart
Your heavy stone heart pulls you down
And over your heavy head, the stars
Scroll in the distance, from east to west
Stars scroll from north to south, stars from
Beginning to end scroll over every heavy stone.

The villages now are sparse and scattered,
And guarded. They live there, new people

People who never saw a lion
Lion who never saw a lion

Now inside a secret
With your face sheared away
Now inside a skeleton
With stars overhead
You bed down."

Never mind anyone
I caution you in high style
I caution you in low style
Seven atrocity figures
Wore doll mask
At a distance

And I pushed over a tree on them

And called the police on them

Many, many police cruisers
Were identical
Surrounding and pointing themselves at something

Seven something, a bundle of tense fibers, actuated
Inside the doll mask
At the very tip of a tree with no branches

It rubbernecked it

| 360°
| 360°

(*optional*)

In all likelihood, in all likelihood, in all likelihood, in all likelihood
Everything was brand new
Everything was like magma
Nothing brought drought
Everything was like water
Everything made hungry
Everything made lunch

(optional)

A hurricane came and caused the land to open.
Also fire, pestilence, and benevolent compassion.
Much later there was a terrible car accident.
Whatever or whatever climbed out of the wreck alive.
Oh well, you know? Everything is ready.
Everything is a receptive sensor.

You'll Be Alone Someday

I've written elsewhere about crystal structure.
I've written elsewhere about flower structure
and caution, and I've written on basic bravery
in flower structures. I've written in confusion
instances of dyslexia among our basic flowers.

I've studied the structure of simple flowers,
improving a guidebook of basic flowers,
decisions of basic flower structure, and
basically one-decision decision systems.
I've written extensively on this elsewhere.
For me it is a primary passion: the daisy,

the raspberry flower. I've grown into a study
of the less intricate flowers. I've seen
the end of flowers. I've matched up diagrams,
the flowers match up with the diagrams.
I think I like the simple flowers the best.
When it rains, don't set the camera flash to On.

...blue daisies, white daisies, buttercups...
These are idiot, these are clover flowers
which are idiot simple when abstracted.
These have never been presented in this way.
They've been frozen in liquid nitrogen
but they are as simple as live flowers

but the subject will be blistered over!
These aren't the epiphytic baroque
deep in the rainforest thirty feet overhead.
These overflow the meadows,
you can find lots of material on them.

The Tree That Has No Reference to the Horizon

They wrap their model of the universe around
Until the water overflows the horizon.

The tree doesn't fit that and stays put.
They walk on it but never discover it.
One of the suits of armor from the boat
Falls empty, clanging, and a rabbit hops out.
It is an imperceptible event

One of the suits of armor from the boat
Is clasped around a different tree trunk all of a sudden and the men laugh

And in the morning they find the horizon
And run along it, laughing and singing in Spanish.

~ ~ ~

Lodged in a tree of smile teeth
Ensnared in the branches of teeth
With legs kicking laughing trying
To get free, a rabbit
Scrambling to get free.

The tree that casts no shadow
The tree that preys upon parasites

No one is content to tell the right joke
No people is happy where they are.
No tree hosts nothing

Or, this tree hosts only a simple smile not its own smile
A laugh that casts no laugher's shadow

It's as always night
As it is always day
And the discoverers row over from the old (this) world
To the sky-filling laughter of this tree

Two Autumns (a "Gates of Hell")

When I cross the following
threshold the leaves will be
gone.
When I cross the following
threshold the leaves will be
gone
and out will come
from the transparent
gates
swirls cut into
parts, pine needle
leaf stem leaf
teeth and tongue
shapes, out comes
a wave and knowledge
fire and
not hot,
a pouring
upside down fire
is knowledge
The writing should respond
to the challenges of different
money
The writing should respond
to the challenges of different

money.
This land is cursed,
the country you
built is a curse,
your money digests
you And
do you know
who I am
I say and they
had answered the
door. My transparent eyes
brought them, standing
between the pillars
of their extremely
expensive home
and my message
It must have the
arrow sound forthrightness the
music arrow arrow
It must have the
arrow sound forthrightness the
music arrow arrow
music as
simple as what
ever it's for, knifing
message down the
sneering, sewn-eye
oil portraits, the
chandelier

smash
No—it must be the wrench
of our lives—the threshold
selects itself
No—it must be the wrench
of our lives—the threshold
selects itself
in fact you
must be out of my
way now, I sit
center in the
ballroom and channel
and repeat and affix
the neutrality of
the yes, the
conviction of the
no, destruction
of property
Halfway between here and the
problems to solve I think
Halfway between here and the
problems to solve I think
speak gushing
here forward
in one transparent
blast, the sort of
wave and water
glass face of
the wave that

pushes through
one
as it shoves
the wealthy owners
of the site aside
and holds
them away
—but I don't
care you're crazy—and
hunger
—but I don't
care you're crazy—and
hunger
Pick a threshold. Disseminable
mantra say on a playing card
serves.
Pick a threshold. Disseminable
mantra say on a playing card
serves
a threshold, a money-free bubble
whose mass and force
frightens them and they
retreat from it. Music
alone in the head hungry.
What you need,
retreat from it. Music
alone in the head hungry.
What you need,
Jacob's ladder

peopled with demons
is the music.
Jacob's ladder
peopled with demons
is the music
scorched on their
faces, diminishment
to be seen or
to look at
in the mirror,
uprising
gargoyles. Turning
Leaf transform the gift of
life
Leaf transform the gift of
life
and
leaves, disappearance
yellow leaf
and
leaves, disappearance
yellow leaf
crosses all of
chaos on a
tightrope
riding a chance
wind, a blast
a chance redirects him
and he lands

on the earth
Tightrope walker between
two trees with leaves
falling all around him
Tightrope walker between
two trees with leaves
falling all around him
He arrives
and the highway
is paved behind him
with fallen demons.
A wind
scours the city
and the leaves
clatter, and
the gates clatter,
flora mourns its
self, the leaves, the
yellow leaves, the
clatter against the
hard foundation of
the site, the leaves
clatter against
unyielding ground,
the leaves flap lost
in a perfect
mirrored maze.

Clock

Is this cuckoo gliding backwards
into its clock
what I look like
to the cuckoo gliding backwards
into its clock
or what the cuckoo gliding backwards
into its clock
looks like
to the cuckoo gliding backwards
into its clock?
Learn a language
and die. Night cuckoo
separates life
from death. Night cuckoo
learn a life language

To chant is a cyclops into
chant is a cyclops in.

To change in a cyclops is to
change in a cyclops is.

and die
hugged in a wing hug
held gliding backwards
into its clock.

Priscilla Lioness

Freeze freeze & refreeze the
creator body, get at his finger
The finger with the __spark__ frozen
at its tip, bite off
The finger and re-freeze The
boddy, bite the ___find the joint___
Lioness carnivore teeth shear the
stump, re-freeze the finger, blow
frost over the spark, bite
away the sparkk.
from the fingertip. Mouth
toss finger aside Mouth
open your teeth mouth & suspend
the spark so it doesn't DEADLY
touch your mouth Priscilla
The spark spitted on a stick
stuck through your cheeks
Black solvents drip from your chin
The spark perfectly encircled not touching

The women the spark birthed were Named lionesses
left on a depopulated plain with only each other
who emptied exhaled death on everyone
squatted over them & laid eggs in their mouths.

Live Priscilla battle Necrotic Priscilla
for imaginary control of a third
uncoupled brass Priscilla zebra horse's
head with the lionessness grafted on at
the eyes to end life, gaze
To grend up the lives brass
head hyanked off some magic
Zebra & battled over, opposing Priscillae
lunging against one another at the
Point of impact
Where the teeth touch
Gaze through upturned zebra ribs

can still see the true Priscilla
stalking between the trees
stalking inside outside a
spreading zebra corpse, a clearing

She turned time traveler inward
and is arriving
She tore apart and swallowed she
and is arriving arriving a special set
of internal teeth turned many angles
coat her internal skin
Rocks outcrop depopulated plain

But I can still see true prior Priscilla
through the bars of a recurrent forest dream
(I am a hourse in the dream)
The trees are false, legs false
I see a lioness head slick with black blood
From hollowing out a zebra's belly

I see the chase against the horizon
Leaps onto her prey, claw needles
Death oil she tears the grazing leaking
apart & severs its talisman head
& wears its spark head, she oversteps
the horizon line in human foarm
Priscilla death Priscilla
the death the angel
of unauthorized death the shearing
surfaces meeting badly en
closing sound chamber You
wear a mask for there to be anything
there THERE at the end of the alleyway
so you can hear the screams
Someone else's scream, a long

A long alleyway with nothing
to the right or the lefft
and you at both ends

Heart like a glassed-in cube of ribcages
on rails On the move
They had been murdered
So they pretended to be about to
be murdered and while Priscilla
was lying railed there pretending
her blood turned into Priscilla and
Priscilla locked the Priscilla inside
Priscilla's heart with her hair
and a box of white chalk
for drawing mouth sentences
from beyond murder

On a list which goes in the eyes and
comes out the mouth the mouth
obeys the chop-up list

body made of ice cream
worm made of ice body
four-legged worm
coating the inside of a lioness
six-legged worm
a trillion legs
crammed into a long ditch
sunk underground and become a tunnel

A long list of blanks for name
The mouth obeys the blanks the blanks
name you Priscilla the blank of
blanks seeds blanks

Each body drops two carcasses
Each carcass yields two corpses
A building full of dead accountants
slides across the empty page

Who put sentences right there,
Who fill in so many of the blanks there are,
Robbing the great libraries and the great anti-libraries,
Obliterating both,
Thin-sectioning ambered embryos,
Shuffling them in with fly slices,
Putting tiny clones in cloned blanks,
Putting tiny stars at tip of fingertip blanks,
So many blanks are just a snap off the fingers,
An insect move,
To fill a blank,
Mold a moment,
A closing of the fingers,
A parting of the teeth,
A frequency
To turn present-day
Humans into half-remembered imperatives
A lack of monuments, single horizons
(here/there/here/there)

The blood travels through time and time,
The pride brings a gazelle resonance
Crashing down to the horizon

Who peels away from
And devours reflection
Echo
Its twin third head

Opens its heart at the seams,
Internal mouths lick the heart seams,
Other Priscillae climb into those mouths,
Stand on the inner surface
Of the planetary crust,
Reversing and pinpointing where up is,
And trains circle the inner surface
Crisscrossing and zigzagging
And other Priscillae step out onto platforms
Out of trains full of Priscilla minnows
Grown to full size,
Trains with tracks on top, driving on top
Of trains with tracks on top,

Jump in front of a train,
The train opens its mouth and swallows,
Travel by worm, make plans for the future,
mother/mother/mother/etc
Rabbit legs, coiled to strike,
Spring with big muscles attached,
Bullet burst speed coiled up extraready,
Grasshopper legs, with too many articulations
Too many,
A viper packed with legs,
An inside-out centipede,
Fang-legs absolutely every cubic inch

Time travel in two places at once

I'll need to get my teeth fixed

Malocclusion in one place at once

etk etk etk etk*
revisiting never

---

* clack the teeth together four times
  traveler

The TV show keeps on broadcasting
A show of dismemberment
At or in between the joints
The arms fingers flex & unflex
Unconnected keep on and keep on
A holy fire that leaps up from the ground
And leaves the galaxy at the speed of light
The stars eat her body on the air
And reassemble, pin her together at the joints
Sharp eternally painful pins of light
create the blanks a story would fill
Would have filled
Her headless body gives birth
from a steadily dilating neck
Streams of hawkscreaming monsters
With Priscillae for second spines
Rain down among the Leonids
Growing stalks from their backs and
Sending legs down to meet the ground
Continuing to meet the ground in greater numbers
Boar and sow worms w/ Priscilla-lizard consciences
Rut and tunnel the land
And lay clusters of empty eggs
In disbelief

Frankenstein's women who sing an inside-out melody
Whose throats are haunted by stairwells' throats
To form the buzz-golemesses of speech
Speech insects rub legs together who
Make use of the stairwell but never the stairs
To fill the stairwell with legs

There is no other melody, only
concentric oral structures propagating
the mythic broadcast medium
resonances and lionesses
a series of satellite dishes of ascending size
to capture outcoming transmissions
forced in sideways at all angles
Into already pointillism body between
ribs from a medical standpoint
the idiots.
Train a satellite dish on death body?
See, it makes no sense.

Thistleheads grinding up feet razors
Grinding up through the concrete
full thistleheads spinning up
grinding up through the soles of the
feet shoving down through the concrete
Grinder heads tearing feet apart &
splintering leg bones sucking blood down

Inks pour from her mouth corners solvent

Razor petals
Razor sepals & leaves spin
Shoved up on stalks through the pavement

Trudge, murdered populace
Trudge
Shove your feet down
through the pavement
Trudge on your way somewhere

Trudging ground up
Legs through

Instructions foarm finite flowerheads
Split here grow there impact
in between
Take dictation, matter
A spark to make mayhem absolute

No algorithm of thistles
Chews themselves up blood ink
Body (made make) ink
But do NOT store ink bodily
for any reason

These shoes are designed to __wear__   __out__ .
Out comes out faster than forced in
The word can't be a compositional unit
in the construction of the Angel of Death
whose body & presence drain words away
From where they are
Razor.
up a person, their relation to gravity
Razor up the field of people
Two words that mean one tarsal
One word that means two teeth
A two-word phrase _____   __heart__ .
That hovering indecision
When presented with a choice of words
Won't be a compositional unit written
On walls where the public can see them
Scoured away from where they are
Walled away. Graffiti in the cheek
of a trudging prey animal
the mouth obeys.

Creator creates a __fem le__   __n me__
Who bites the fingertip off
To create herself, haunted by
flesh not description Frankenstein the book
Haunted by material. Narration
of one's actions is monstrous. It
brings itself to construct a murderous woman
of algorithms, pre-algorithms, chance procedures,
pages and pages she said all along
what she was doing she didn't think

Polar animals skid to a halt
wearing white, useless bodies,
liabilities in a green expanse.

Dump everything everyone out
Disgorge time traveler
on a greenish plain where
one doesn't belong
made of teeth tiny outcroppings. Disgorge
not anything that's you, though.

Egg lives in names[1].
Egg[2] Y/N name[3].
Lives[4] give method[5].
Horror[6] has no opposite[7].
Horror[8] Y/N method[9].
Y/N spells shape[10],
Revision[11] loves algorithm[12],
Mayhem[13] loves revision[14],
Blanks outcrop,
Algorithms[15] become names[16],
Mayhem[17] loves names[18],
Mayhem[19] Y/N shape[20],
Algorithm[21] does translate,
Absolute something[22] is female[23],
Melody[24] comes in a hard eggshell[25]
From improvisation or not improvisation.
Melody names itself[26]—herself[27].
Same with egg[28]—ighuman[29].

---

1. Or, algorithms.
2. Or, names.
3. Or, mayhem.
4. Or, names.
5. Or, mayhem.
6. Or, shape.
7. Or, algorithm.
8. Or, translation.
9. Or, something.
10. Or, female.
11. Or, melody.
12. Or, eggshell.
13. Or, itself.
14. Or, herself.
15. Or, names.
16. Or, egg(s).
17. Or, name.
18. Or, lives.
19. Or, method.
20. Or, horror.
21. Or, opposite.
22. Or, horror.
23. Or, method.
24. Or, shape.
25. Or, revision.
26. Or, algorithm.
27. Or, mayhem.
28. Or, revision.
29. Or, egg(s).

Try to tell a cosmos-ending angel how to have been composed.
The sound of the search for the compositional unit
As if sound could sever the sounding vocal cords.
A nuanced account
Oneself never oneself at a frequency of
Construction of a careful and correct understanding
Of a dismemberment goddess
Out of oneself. A suture pulled
Made of units, not thread. Undone
A lioness head with roar gurgling out
Pinned under a death-angel lioness head's foot
So it won't flutter away
Into (human-readable) image
Out of an image.